Epic Cars

Corvette Z06

D1736826

JULIA GARSTECKI

BLACK
RABBIT
BOOKS

Bolt is published by Black Rabbit Books
P.O. Box 3263, Mankato, Minnesota, 56002.
www.blackrabbitbooks.com
Copyright © 2020 Black Rabbit Books

Marysa Storm, editor; Catherine Cates,
interior designer; Grant Gould, cover designer;
Omay Ayres, photo researcher

Library of Congress Cataloging-in-Publication Data
Names: Garstecki, Julia, author.
Title: Corvette Z06 / by Julia Garstecki.
Description: Mankato, Minnesota : Black Rabbit Books, [2020] | Series: Bolt.
Epic cars | Audience: Age 9-12. | Audience: Grade 4 to 6. |
Includes bibliographical references and index.
Identifiers: LCCN 2018018970 (print) | LCCN 2018019798 (ebook) |
ISBN 9781680728422 (e-book) | ISBN 9781680728347 (library binding) |
ISBN 9781644660331 (paperback)
Subjects: LCSH: Corvette automobile–Juvenile literature.
Classification: LCC TL215.C6 (ebook) | LCC TL215.C6 G37 2020 (print) |
DDC 629.222/2–dc23
LC record available at https://lccn.loc.gov/2018018970

Special thanks to Owen Parker for his help with this book.

Printed in the United States. 1/19

Image Credits

BOLT

Contents

 Racing Down the Road

The driver pushes the start button. The Chevrolet Corvette Z06 comes to life. The car takes off. Roaring, its body cuts through the wind. It zips through curves effortlessly.

Chevy built the Z06 for the street. But the car's power makes it perfect for the track.

1953

2015

Incredible Power

The first Corvette came out in 1953. It amazed drivers. In 2015, a redesigned Z06 hit the streets. The car is smooth. It's sleek. The Z06 shares features with the C7.R race car. Like the race car, the Z06 is powerful and fast.

The Z06 can come as a convertible.

FENDERS

FRONT SPLITTER

WIDE, LOW BODY

SPOILER

WHEELS

CHAPTER 2

Design

The Z06's design makes it stand out. Its shape also makes it **aerodynamic**. Designers built it to cut through air. Its shape creates **downforce** too. Downforce makes cars stable at high speeds.

Three Features that Create
Downforce

FRONT SPLITTER

SPOILER

HOOD VENT

Staying Cool

Design features help the Z06 stay cool. They keep the car from **overheating**. The grille brings fresh air to the engine. The vent on the hood lets hot air out.

Fenders

The Z06 has wide fenders. They make the car look wide and low. They also make room for wider tires. Wider tires give cars more grip. More grip makes it easier for cars to stop and turn.

Some parts, such as the hood, are made from **carbon fiber**. Carbon fiber is strong but light.

Personalizing

Buyers can personalize their Z06s.
They have 10 exterior colors to choose
from. Buyers can also add stripes
or **decals**. Inside, most Z06s
are black. Buyers can order
gray or red seats.

MANY OPTIONS

Buyers have many options when getting their 2019 Z06s.

10
EXTERIOR COLORS

12
STRIPES AND DECALS

7
WHEEL OPTIONS

2

SEAT OPTIONS

• • • • • • **4**

BRAKE CALIPER
COLORS

4

ROOF
OPTIONS

BASE PRICES

$100,000		
$80,000		
$60,000		
$40,000		
$20,000		
0		

Price

1LZ — $79,495

2LZ — $83,060

3LZ — $88,440

Trim Packages

Buyers can choose from three trim packages. Each trim package has special features. The 1LZ is the basic package. It includes power seats and a backup camera. With the 2LZ, drivers get heated and vented seats. It has more cameras too. The 3LZ comes with all that and more.

CHAPTER 3

Power and Performance

The Z06's power comes from a **supercharged** 6.2-liter V-8 engine. The engine makes 650 **horsepower**. The Z06 can reach 60 miles (97 kilometers) per hour in just 2.95 seconds. Its top speed is more than 200 miles (322 km) per hour.

COMPARING HORSEPOWER

Challenger SRT Hellcat

Corvette Z06

Ford GT

horsepower

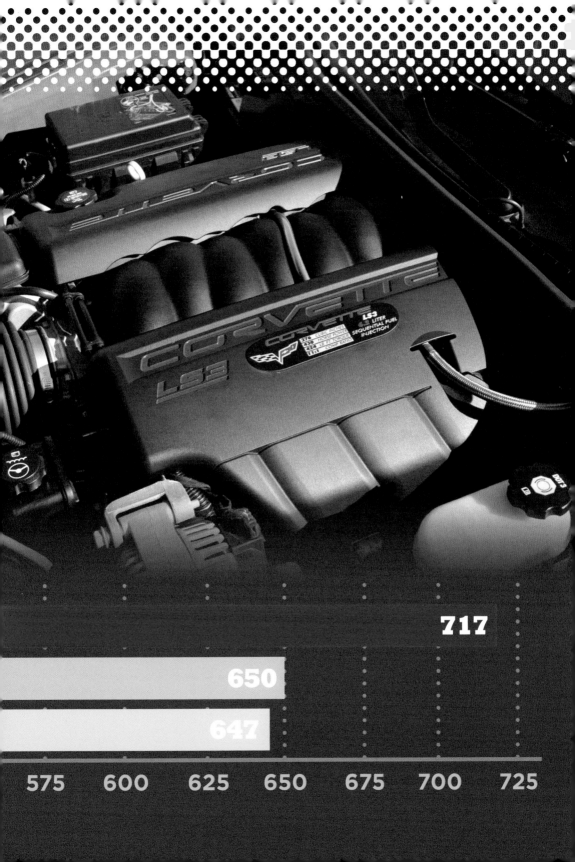

717

650

647

575 600 625 650 675 700 725

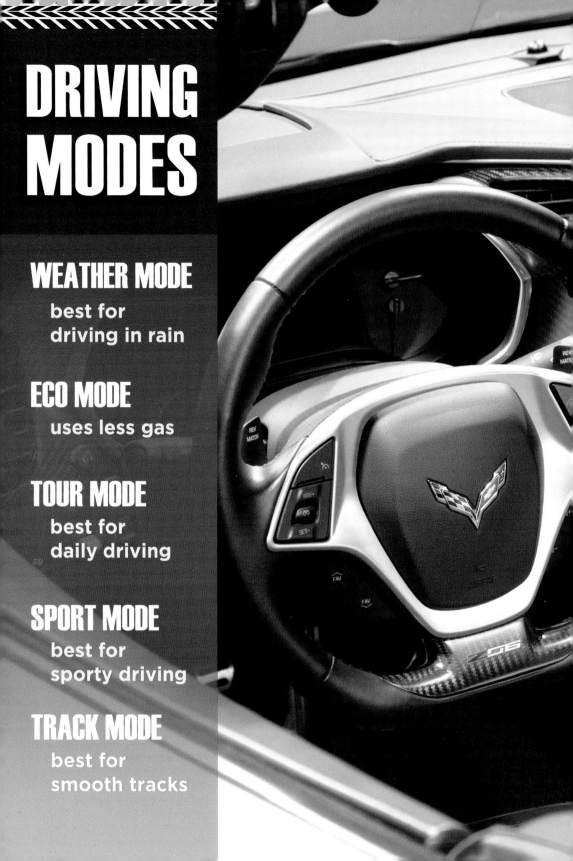

DRIVING MODES

WEATHER MODE
best for driving in rain

ECO MODE
uses less gas

TOUR MODE
best for daily driving

SPORT MODE
best for sporty driving

TRACK MODE
best for smooth tracks

Driving Modes

Drivers can change more than how their Z06s look. They can change how the cars handle. They do this by choosing driving modes. The modes let drivers adjust **traction**, steering, and more.

2

TOTAL SEATING

By the Numbers

3,524
POUNDS
(1,598 KILOGRAMS)
WEIGHT

99.6 FEET (30 meters)
DISTANCE IT TAKES TO STOP FROM SPEED OF **60 MILES** (97 KM) PER HOUR WITH SPECIAL OPTIONS

177.9 INCHES (452 CENTIMETERS) **LENGTH**

ESTIMATED HIGHWAY MILEAGE

about **22** miles (35 km) per gallon

CHAPTER 4

An Epic Car

Many people love the Z06. It is easy to see why. This supercar has good looks. It reaches high speeds. Corvettes have amazed drivers for years. And they will thrill drivers for many more.

aerodynamic (air-oh-dahy-NAM-ik)—something that is shaped so it moves easily through air

caliper (KAL-uh-per)—a device used to press a brake pad against the sides of a brake rotor

carbon fiber (KAR-buhn FAHY-bur)—a very strong, lightweight material

decal (DEE-kal)—a picture, design, or label that will stick to the surface on which it is placed

downforce (doun-FAWRS)—a force that increases the stability of a motor vehicle by pressing it downward

horsepower (HORS-pow-uhr)—a unit used to measure the power of engines

mileage (MAHY-lij)—the average number of miles a vehicle will travel on a gallon of gasoline

overheat (o-vuhr-HET)—to become too hot

spoiler (SPOI-ler)—a device placed on a vehicle to reduce lift and increase drag; it "spoils" airflow.

supercharged (SOO-pur-chahrjd)—for an engine to have a device that brings more air to the engine

traction (TRAK-suhn)—the adhesive friction of a body on a surface on which it moves, such as a tire on the road

BOOKS

Cruz, Calvin. *Chevrolet Corvette Z06*. Car Crazy. Minneapolis: Bellwether Media, Inc., 2016.

Jacobs, David H. *Corvette: The Classic American Sports Car*. Speed Rules! Inside the World's Hottest Cars. Broomall, PA: Mason Crest, 2018.

Piddock, Charles. *Chevy Corvette*. Vroom! Hot Cars. Vero Beach, FL: Rourke Educational Media, 2016.

WEBSITES

2019 Corvette Z06: Sports Car
www.chevrolet.com/performance/corvette-z06-sports-car

Chevrolet Corvette Z06
www.caranddriver.com/chevrolet/corvette-z06

Road Atlanta: Corvette Racing's Tommy Milner Takes the Z06 for a Hot Lap | Chevrolet
www.youtube.com/watch?v=VmrPPBrZZ7c

INDEX